Basic Music Theory

A Beginner's Guide
Volume 1

By Seol Kyung Bae
Design By Andrew Kim

Copyright © 2018 Seol Kyung Bae
All Rights Reserved

ISBN-13: 978-1987521474
ISBN-10: 1987521471

No part of this book may be reproduced
without written permission from the author.

TABLE OF CONTENTS

Introduction 3
Drawing Clefs 4
Circle of Fifths 6
Key Signature 8
Crossword Puzzle 10
Time Signature 12
Reading Notes 14
Review of Key Signatures and Notes 16
Coloring 18
Answer Key 20
Staff Paper 22

INTRODUCTION

Welcome to Basic Music Theory, the very first non-boring music theory book! We will be working on the fundamentals of music. The purpose of this book is to introduce and teach all young musicians that music theory can be engaging. Through crossword puzzles, coloring, and mix and matching, first time theory learners will have a friendlier and pleasant experience. Hope you little musicians are ready to have some fun!

Seol Kyung Bae

Drawing Clefs

In this section, we will be learning how to draw different clefs in music and learn which basic instruments use the clef as their main domain.

Treble Clef (G-Clef): The clef for the higher register instruments.
Instruments: Piano, Violin, Flute, Recorder

Bass Clef (F-Clef): The clef for the lower register instruments.
Instruments: Piano, Cello, Bassoon

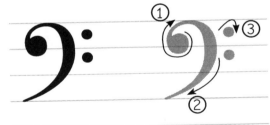

Alto Clef (C-Clef): The clef for the middle register instruments.
Instruments: Viola, Cello, Bassoon

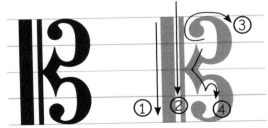

Now, practice drawing the clefs on the staves below!

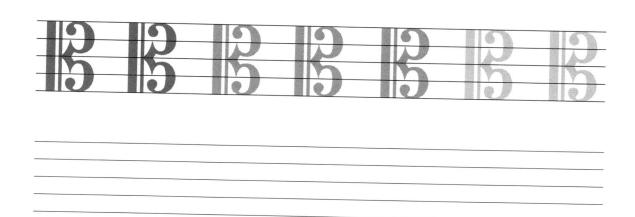

Circle of Fifths

In this section, we will be going over how many sharps and flats are in each Major Key.

Numbers inside the circle represent how many sharps and flats are in each major key. The name of the Major Keys are represented on the outside.

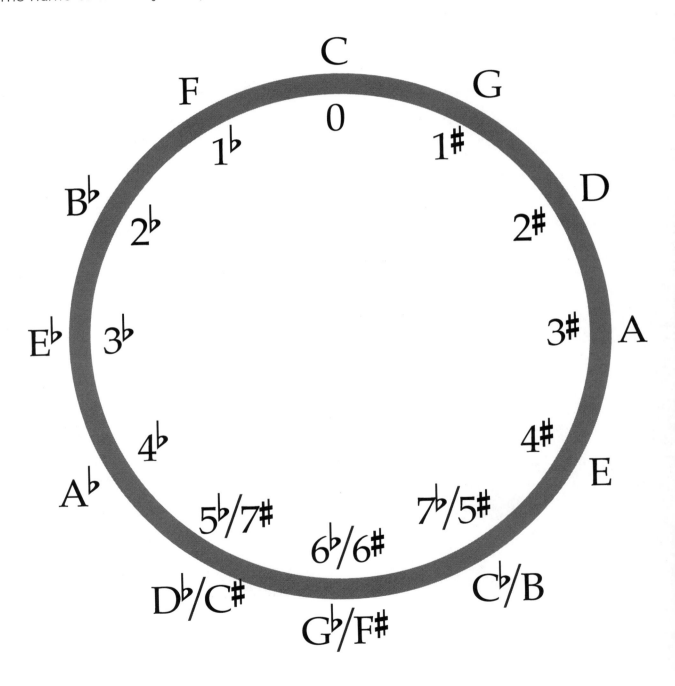

Order of Sharps

F♯ C♯ G♯ D♯ A♯ E♯ B♯

My favorite acronym to remember the order of sharps is
Follow Clouds Going Down And Enjoy Bowling.

Think of your own acronym or phrase for **F C G D A E B** and write it below!

Order of Flats

B♭ E♭ A♭ D♭ G♭ C♭ F♭

For the order of flats, I use
BEAD and **G**reatest **C**ommon **F**actor.

Think of your own: **B E A D G C F** and write it below!

KEY SIGNATURE

In this section, we will learn key signature by placing sharps and flats, and naming major keys. Draw the sharp(s) or the flat(s) on the staff, and write down the name of the major key. Look back at the Circle of Fifths on page 6 to check your answers!

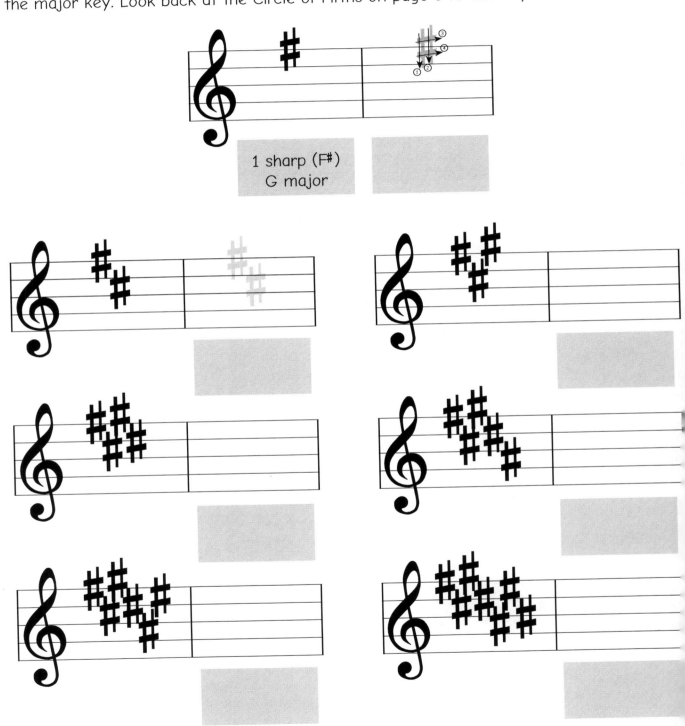

☆REMEMBER☆: When you draw the sharp/flats and the notes onto the staff, remember that they have to be exactly between the lines or in the middle of the line.

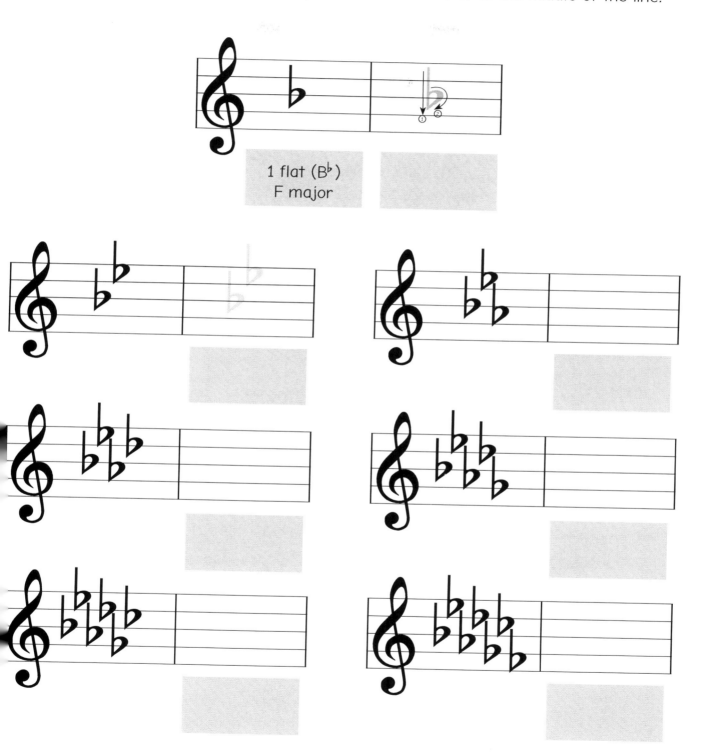

CROSSWORD PUZZLE

Instruction: In this section, we will be having some fun with different musical terms and different instruments! Ready to play some crossword puzzles?

WORD BANK: FLATS, TREBLE, PIANO, FORTE, BASS, SHARPS, ALTO

ACROSS
1. To play softly
3. The high register clef: G-Clef
7. Looks similar to a lowercase "b"

DOWN
2. To play loudly
4. The middle register clef: C-Clef
5. Looks similar to a hashtag

DIAGONAL
6. The lower register clef: F-Clef

WORD BANK:
VIOLA, DOUBLE BASS, VIOLIN, CELLO, PIANO

ACROSS
1. The lowest voice and the biggest of the string family
4. Soprano voice of the string family

DOWN
2. A large keyboard instrument
3. Second biggest in the string family
5. Middle voice of the string family

Time Signature

In this section, we will be going over how to read time signatures.

Before we go ahead and learn how to read the time signature, let's go over some basic note value.

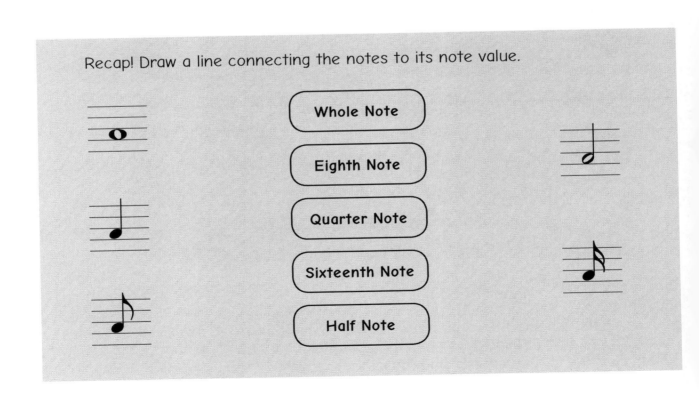

Now we are going to go ahead and learn how to read and understand time signature.

4/4

The top number tells us "how many beats" there are in a measure.

The bottom number tells us "which note gets the single beat." This 4 stands for Quarter Note. Therefore, a single quarter note is one beat.

SIDE NOTE

  4/4 can also be represented as Common Time. The symbol for Common Time is similar to the letter "C".

3/4
Read as: Three Four
Top Number: Three Beats in each measure.
Bottom Number: One Quarter Note gets one beat out of the three beats.

6/8
Read as: Six Eight
Top Number: Six Beats in each measure.
Bottom Number: One Eighth Note gets one beat out of the six beats.

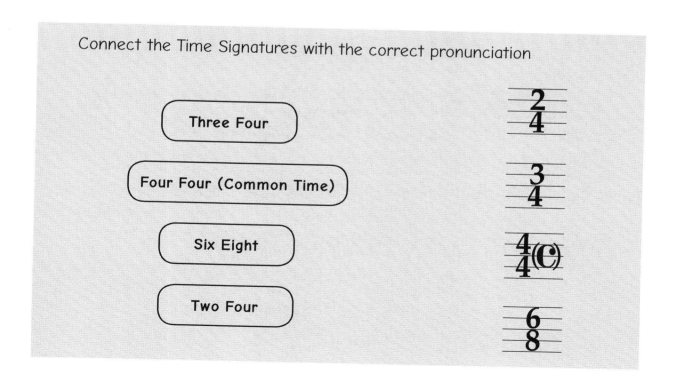

Connect the Time Signatures with the correct pronunciation

- Three Four
- Four Four (Common Time)
- Six Eight
- Two Four

2/4, 3/4, 4/4 (C), 6/8

Reading Notes

In this section, we will be learning how to read basic notes and see where they are placed on the staff lines.

When we read notes, we always read our notes from **bottom up**! Always remember!

SPACE NOTES

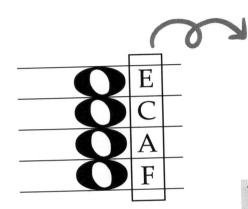

What word does it spell out? **F.A.C.E**!
These are the first four space notes that we learn in music.

Think of your own and write it down here!

LINE NOTES

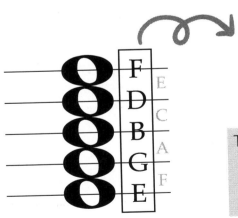

Unfortunately, line notes do not spell out a word. But we can come up with a phrase to remember!
Ex: **E**ggs **G**et **B**urnt **D**uring **F**rying.

Think of your own and write it down here!

Now we are going to put all of our notes together!

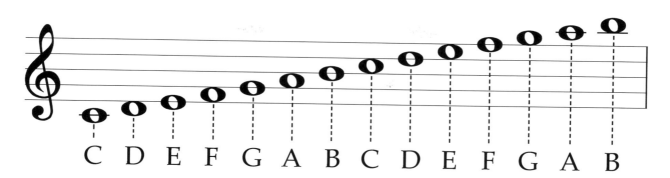

There are only 7 unique notes we need to remember in music: **C D E F G A B**
Notes are repeated in different registers and octaves.

Now let's practice reading notes. Down below are some examples of notes. Go ahead and identify them.

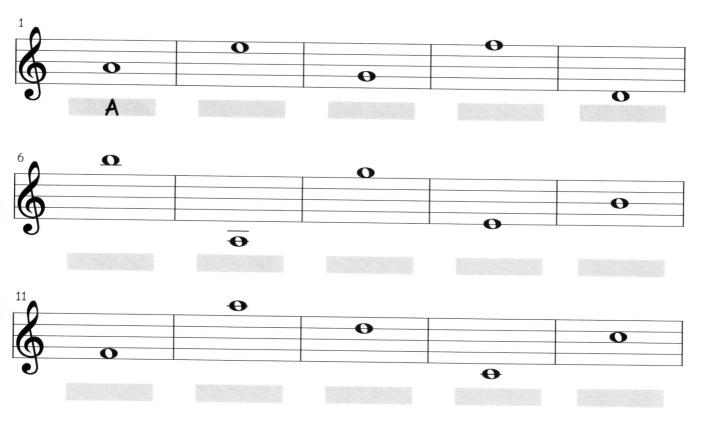

Key Signatures & Notes

More Practice
Please write down the names of the sharps/flats and identify the Key Signatures below.

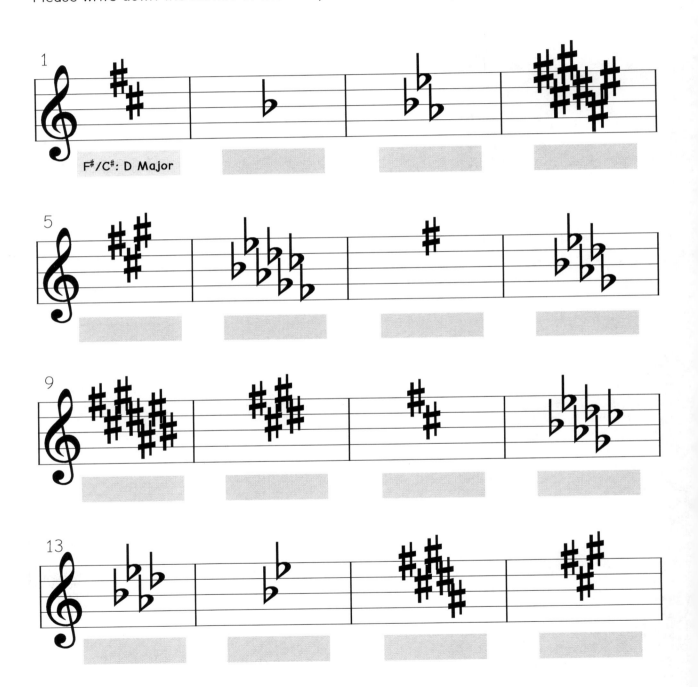

Please write down the names of the notes below.

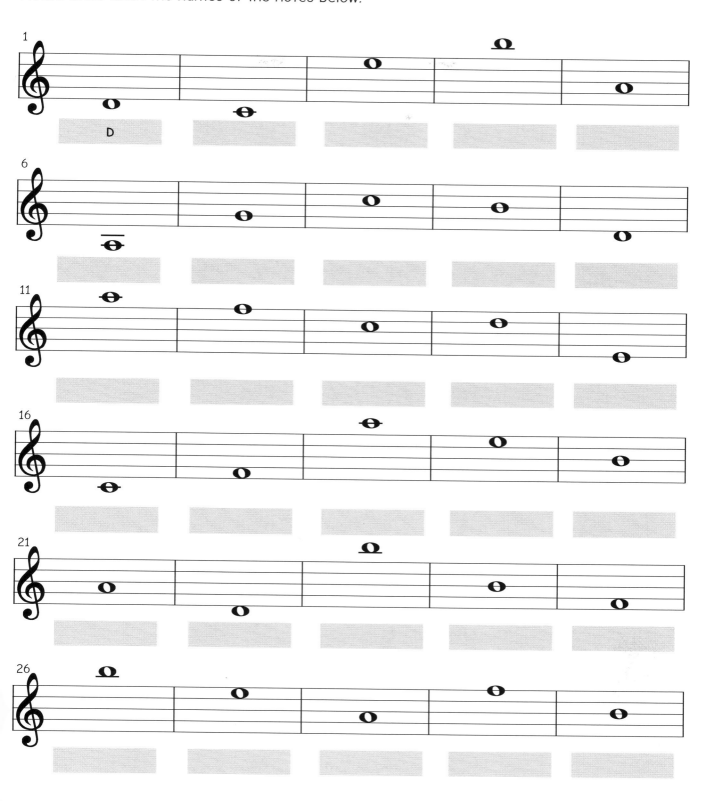

COLORING

Time for some fun!

Answer Key

Page 10-11

Page 12-13

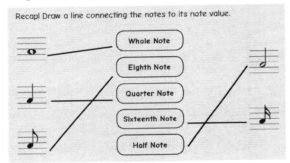

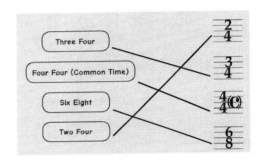

Page 15

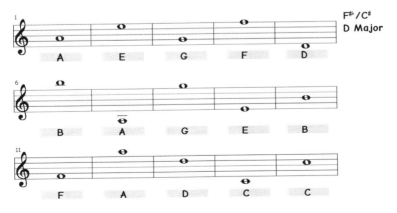

Page 16

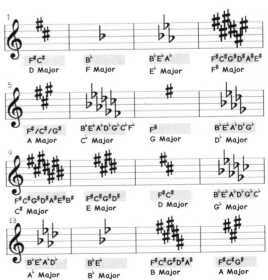

Page 17

Staff Paper

Enjoy!

Made in the USA
Middletown, DE
11 December 2018